HEALING
with
COLOR

Published by Empower Productions, Inc.
500 Brookeshyre Court
Woodstock, GA 30188

First printing: January 2006

Library of Congress: 2006900693

ISBN: 0-9711150-5-2

Printed in China through Four Colour Imports

Pencil Illustrations and Cover Photograph by Mande Porter
Illustration Color and Book Design by Jill Balkus
Edited by Tara Green

HEALING
with
COLOR

Seeing & Feeling
The Glorious Power of Color

Carolyn Porter, D. Div.

Empower Productions, Inc.

Also by Carolyn Porter

❧ Books ❧

A Woman's Path to Wholeness: The Gift is in the Process

*The Realness of a Woman: A Journey for Seeking, Remembering &
Being Who You Are*

Healing with Color: Seeing & Feeling the Glorious Power of Color

❧ Ebooks ❧

Put the Dynamo in Your Communication

Stress Free Living

❧ Audios ❧

Grab Your Authentic Power

Healthier & Younger: Turn Back the Clock

Healing With Color

This gift from the angels is given for the souls who choose the path of divine enlightenment to illuminate their healing. To every being on this planet who desires to return to wholeness.

From the Angels

We are giving you this healing advancement so that you can see the endless possibilities of creating truth in the midst of darkness. The darkness lies within the recesses of your physical being, your thoughts, and your feelings. Only the Light of God can heal that darkness. We are giving you the beauty of color—in this you can be whole.

See the colors before your eyes, and we will again teach you how to feel. You do not take time to feel, especially to love, because of the mindlessness and pain in your world. You bring in sickness, sickness in your physical being, your thoughts, and your heart. You bury the feelings, rushing here to there, and do not understand the beauty. We want to teach you how to feel love so that you can be love.

Thoughts to My Readers

The angels have shared the gift of their masterpiece through me so that I can share it with you. It is priceless. The words that are on these pages are from their loving whispers, for they are aware of our pain; they sprinkle loving angel dust upon us to wash away the pain. They want us to feel love and peace so that we will lift up the consciousness of the planet. People are seeking, asking, and shifting because the angels are stirring them. It is time for realness, and it is in the awareness of the real moment we feel. Through the texture and feeling of the colors that the angels have channeled through me, you can understand the power of love deep within your heart, awakening your physical being and your thoughts with pure truth. The truth is already inside you, hidden beneath the darkness that shadows your life. Breathe deeply as you quietly allow Divine Light to encircle your soul with love and allow you to return to wholeness.

With Deepest Appreciation

So it is, with the deepest feeling of appreciation, that I gratefully acknowledge the messages, support, and divine guidance of the angels, archangels and ascended masters, for they shine a brilliant light for me, as well as you, in order that our lives can be raised into the highest vibration of abundance, peace, and wholeness through the expression of love.

To my children—Stephen, Deborah, Scott, Melinda and Mande—
and the expression of love we share.

To all family members and the gift each one brings to my life.

To my team, Tara and Pete, who willingly and lovingly raise me into
higher realms of awareness and love.

To my daughter Mande, for sharing her artistic gift with a loving
heart as she created into life the beautiful angels in this book.

To my designer Jill, whose creativity and talent has brought into
reality the vision I was given for this writing.

Table of Contents

Foreword

Open up to the gifts from the angels; they are miracles. Reach out your hand and your heart for the angels give them to you. The gift of color is a precious gift through which you can learn to feel the beauty that lies within each of you and reaches the far corners of the world, expressing through every being that lives. There are no sorrows or hurts that cannot be healed by the feelings in the celestial colors as they intertwine the souls of those who desire healing. Reach out and gently swirl the colors to you, as divine light touches your heart, pouring love through every cell in your physical being. Allow this gift to envelope you, reaching beyond the dimension of your knowingness, and feel divine peace and healing with the footprints of love.

We left our home and are traveling our paths to experience this life and the lessons we need to learn. We are always seeking the way home through our expansion into higher dimensions. As we vibrate into higher realms we free ourselves to expand our soul. We need not remain attached to our disorders, if they be physical, emotional, mental or spiritual. But letting go has been difficult for us all.

The angels are ever with us, guiding, loving, protecting and encouraging. We may not be aware of their presence, but they are there. It is because they love us so that they are showering us with the gift of healing colors. Imagine sprinkles of angel dust in beautiful celestial colors illuminating the sky as they float gently into us, gracing us with pure love. Only love heals, and through the colors we can learn to love . . . then heal.

Love is in the feeling of each real moment. Love is in the silence where Spirit speaks. Love is in still moments in time where nothing else exists. Feel that love. Bring it into your heart and let it expand, permeating your entire being. Love is all there is, and when you can feel love radiating through every cell, you can heal. This is the knowingness that the angels are giving. Feel the love through the beauty of the colors.

Through this book you will experience an awareness for life that you may have forgotten or perhaps never known. Through these colors you can learn to feel in the depths that have eluded you until now. As the gentle whirlwind of colors flow through you, allow the vibrations to waft in and out of every corner and crevice of your being, lifting you up into Divine Perfection.

There are 13 celestial colors shared from the angels, each one with its own divine feeling. Each has its own emotional field of healing, and can touch the soul as one or in succession of the other. The power lies in their essence—Divine Energy—and as we draw that energy through us we know the Power that heals. We are one with that Divine Energy. It is the feeling that experiences the knowingness.

Your journey begins, the journey that heals. The Light will guide you. In the center of the Light are the colors expressed as they burst with magnificent splendor into the realm of your consciousness, opening your heart and soul to the core of your being, aligning to your Divine power. In the space where nothing is, the feeling of these celestial colors transcends your soul to expand the love, and where nothing is but the power of love miracles happen. There abides our healing. Where there is love, there is faith. Faith brings miracles. Miracles happen to those who believe!

About Angels

People often ask questions about angels, "What do they look like?" or "What do they wear?" or "What do they do all the time?" or "Are they really around us?" People ask these questions because they doubt, not that they doubt the existence of angels, but rather they doubt themselves.

So for those who may still doubt, or for those who haven't knowingly experienced angels in their life, let me tell you about angels, God's expression of love.

Angels are pure love. They are by your side at all times and seem to be in many places simultaneously. Their mission is to help you, giving to you in love. Angels never do anything except from love. They will guide you, encourage you, send messages to you, protect you, and sometimes lovingly give you prodding or lessons for growth. Everything they do is for the highest and best for you and others, always given with kindness and compassion.

My Thoughts About Angels

All my life I have believed in angels but my early thoughts were that angels resided in heaven and were near me at certain times to protect me. It wasn't until recent years that I discovered the incredible presence of angels in my life daily, guiding every step I take because I am willing to listen to their messages. As I allowed my awareness of their presence to expand, I am able to see, feel and hear them with complete freedom. The same is open to you. I invite you to receive them into your life and you will be blessed beyond anything that can be measured.

❧ What Do Angels Look Like? ❧

They are beautiful! They glow with the Light of God, for they are of God. They are perfect and give only truth to you. Angels can manifest any color or presence for the moment. They may appear in form for your recognition, but they are not really of body for they are beings of light. They radiate their love and smiling expressions, even when sending us lessons. All comes to you as a beam of love.

❧ What Do Angels Wear? ❧

Their garments are of many colors, fabrics and presences. Sometimes the colors are soft while other times they are vibrant. They don't need garments since they are angels and are encircled in light, but they give you the illusion of garments for you to see. Mostly the garments seem to flow loosely around them. Angels feel color and use every color in the spectrum of the universe. Color is beauty, and through the colors they are giving you, you can see that beauty.

❧ What Do Angels Do? ❧

Angels relate God's messages. They are wonderful listeners and await your requests. Nothing makes them happier than to feel your appreciation for the gifts they have given you, which are endless. They are your instructors and gently teach you with lessons of love. They send love to you in many forms—comforting, supporting, praising, uplifting, warning—always intending to make you smile. They await your prayers for help, for you must ask for their help. When you need more guidance, they will give it. Sometimes they sprinkle angel dust over your sadness for they see your pain. Then they help you bring back a smile.

Angels love to play. They can be silly and laugh too. They playfully wink and sprinkle angel dust. Have you ever seen angels jump across rocks in a stream or play tag? You might be surprised how well they dance too. Their singing voices are exquisite as are all their musical abilities. Angels are not bound by earth's limitations. They enjoy many things you enjoy.

Are Angels Really Around Us?

Angels are ever present. You may not see them or feel their presence, or even hear them speaking, but they are there. Your guardian angels never leave you. With a thought or a blink of an eye, an angelic being is present. You may call on a specific angel for help, perhaps an archangel, or you can ask for a group of angels to assist you in a particular task. Many have seen angelic presences in life-like form; others have seen shadows or bursts of light. Perhaps you've felt a sensation of warmth or a gentle touch, or maybe experienced movement or the feeling of an angel's breath wisp by you. Have you ever seen spots of light? Angels are always around you!

Enlightenments

First Enlightenment

Color is here on earth for your eyes, your heart, your soul, to enhance your life, but you take it for granted. You do not take time to enjoy the beauty of nature or the value of colors that manifest through it. Slow down physical beings, so you understand the realness of life.

Second Enlightenment

Humans think on a linear plane. We are helping you to break that pattern of linear thinking to see the whole sphere of life so you can think in expanded periphery. You are seeking, looking for the breadth, depth and width of life, wanting answers, wanting love, desiring to grasp what lies beyond your present realm of consciousness.

Third Enlightenment

Angels have a universal picture of how to do things. Listen to us and follow our guidance. Your life would flow with more continuity and peacefulness if you listen more. Use your heart as the star that will guide you in the darkness to find the true Light.

Fourth Enlightenment

Human hearts are frozen. The colors will begin to melt away the coldness and allow the rich golden light of love to flow through you. You have forgotten the ecstasy of that love from whence you came, yet continually seek to experience that love. The colors can bring you back to the beauty of that divine, perfect love.

Fifth Enlightenment

Each color is independent of the other and can be used as a separate entity, but when used together in succession, the collective energy makes them even more powerful. There is a reason for the order of the colors as each leads into the next step, but you may choose any color without order. Each color has specific thoughts, feelings, textures and images, each with its own meaning. Experience the colors and you have reached into the heavenly dimension that touches the light of God.

How to Use This Book

Everything in our universe consists of energy from which all living form is created. Energy is always in motion as either a positive or negative force. A law of the universe says that every form of energy sent out will come back in the same form. This knowingness means wherever you focus your energy is where your vibrations align to create what will show up in your life.

People have been conditioned to see through the eyes of negativity so have been creating the opposite of what they truly want in their life. In the quest for what they desire—love, wealth, health, serenity, happiness, fulfillment—they push, shove and drive themselves to produce and achieve more, believing this will bring them the desires of their heart. During this process they have forgotten their essence of love and its expressions, which are how they can bring to them the desires they long for.

The focus of this book is in feelings that uplift the soul to a higher level of awareness in order that the reader can return to his/her original knowingness. Once feelings are attached to a thought it is created into reality. It is the feeling that makes a thought real through the energy that creates it, and by adding color it allows the individual a deeper awareness of it. In nature we see color and feeling represented over and over again.

Many individuals never take notice of these things because their life is too full of the quest for material gain and temporary pleasure. The message in this book is for regaining divine perspective.

Any color can be used for a particular feeling, but through the power of association the angels have given a feeling to a certain color to help the reader better understand through visual and sensual connection. Often an individual needs this connection to make it a reality in their life. The colors with their feelings and associations to nature and this world can allow an individual to see at a higher level in order to release the old negative aspects of their programming and accept the positive aspects of their divine heritage. It is only in this state of divine enlightenment that healing can occur in all dimensions.

Use this book as another way to internalize truths that benefit your life rather than break you down. Meditate with the colors and use the empowering feelings that each color represents to create your true desires, whether it is for healing in your physical body, your mind, your heart or greater spiritual awareness. Focus on these expressions of love to lead you to a higher plane of awareness and enlightenment where you are real. Any challenge is an illusion but most people focus their energy on that situation. By focusing on what is real, which originates in your essence of love, you can allow and accept healing in your life.

Visualizing the Flow of Celestial Colors

And thus we begin healing with the celestial colors. The healing is of the physical being, permeating the emotional realm, entering the mental periphery, as one allows the spiritual oneness with each dimension. There is no separation from these planes, for each alone, and then together, completes the energy circle that separates us from another as it joins us all in collective consciousness. We are one with our Creator as we are one with another, so as one heals we all heal. Our power can be interchanged with focus and intention. So while we can bring this Flow through us for our own healing, we can also send the energy of these colors through the spiritual dimension that unites us in the same energy vibration.

The Visualizing

- Sit quietly, taking deep breaths as you slowly let go. Feel yourself sinking down into the depths of your soul. Allow divine beings to encompass you, folding you in their love.

- Begin by drawing white light through your crown chakra. Feel the power as you pull it within you, gently swirling through your physical being like a tornado in slow motion gracefully descending on the earth. Feel it opening you, gracing you with divine love. Allow it to permeate your entire being as it slowly moves through you, down into the center of the earth, grounding you. Then allow it to come back into your heart center.

- Draw the celestial colors into you through your crown chakra as with the white light. Gently, ever so gently, allow them to meander in a swirling fashion to wherever you want to focus - wherever healing is needed.

- With each color you must open up to feel the color, smell it, touch it with your thoughts, sensing much about that color. It is with the feeling that the color comes alive to you and renews your life cells.

- Direct the softening point of the funnel-shaped color into the blocked space where healing is needed. Allow yourself to feel that color. The feelings are explained in the chapter of that color. There is no mystery with feeling these colors, only remembering. For all that you can do you already know.

There is no expressiveness as to the beauty of these colors unless they are felt. The feeling makes them real. Once you have felt the divine origin of this healing advancement, you will not be the same. As you walk down the path or ride along a road, you will see colors as you've never seen before, because you are aware and feel beyond what the human eye can see. The awareness is all you need to reveal the beauty and depth of life as you have forgotten. As you breathe in this beauty, you too are beautiful, so you can see the beauty all around you.

The colors are successive in the flow, but each can stand alone in its own power. Each color has a gift. The first six celestial colors are for opening, cleansing, healing and seeing beyond. They are for your beingness, to be taken within so you can heal. The next six celestial colors, deeper versions of the first six, are for renewing and vitality as you radiate out to the world and continue the healing. The final celestial color blankets you with "all is in divine perfection." As you feel each color you can shift from your old beliefs that are of lower negative vibrations and by releasing them can allow higher vibrations of loving energy to recharge you and bring you into wholeness.

Hope

The Angel of Lavender

Feel the gentle whirlwind of Lavender

moving deep into the core of your beingness,

bringing faith, the essence of love.

Peacefulness transcends in the eye of the storm

mingling as vapors of amethyst hues.

In this moment you are breaking through

all barriers of time, feeling the oneness

with your Creator.

Precious Hope, my angel guardian,

guiding, supporting and loving me,

through all eternity.

Chapter 1

First Light: Lavender

Gem: Amethyst

Flower: Lilac

Feeling:
Acceptance

*I*n your mind's eye pull to you the soft lavender celestial light. Gently see it swirling as a tornado in slow motion. Its rounded point will enter wherever you direct it as it displays the edgings of dazzling divine white light. This light is embracing you with the power of God, and in this celestial color you can feel your connection to all power and love.

Feel the lavender light bathing your soul as it slowly descends through your being, filling every space of emptiness or pain, cascading and graceful as it reverently spirals into you. Know your oneness with God and feel it transcend you as billowing lavender light. Allow the wealth of the universe to encircle you as you fully accept your majesty to be claimed. Your birthright is of noble standing, worthy as kings and queens. Feel the richness encompass your being as it pours into your life force, mingling, spreading like a vapor as it transcends all space or form.

See deep into your inner core the holiness of this moment as you take into you all gratitude for every experience in your present or past life, and for all that is coming to you now. Be silent and imagine your being in the eye of a storm, totally at peace in the knowing that you are protected from the whirling madness around you. Now let go of all resistance no matter how much it grasps at you, begging you to hang on tight. As the resistance leaves your awareness feel a surge of God's essence filling you to overflowing so that it seems you cannot hold it all, for you can not. Such is the nature of God's infinite love that is free to you at every moment of eternity.

Imagine in your mind's view regally displayed mountains towering in the horizon with varying shades of misty purple hues hovering over them. Sense the power and awesomeness of this beauty as it literally takes away your breath. Feel the power in these creations of splendor, as they rise to reach the endlessness of the sky, seeming as though they are in charge of all that lays below.

Smell the sweet fragrance of lilacs as they gracefully cascade their color and beauty. Soft and delicate, falling in perfect symmetry, their fragrance mingles with the rays of lavender light, spreading through your blood as a rush of royal greatness. Adjust your gaze to the small blossoms of the deep purple violets, peeking up from the lowness of the ground through blades of green foliage as they ever so gently nod their tiny heads in approval of you. Smell the scent of lavender that calms the soul, envisioning sachets of its delicate fragrance encased in fabric etched by simple lace. Accept all that is in perfection.

As the lavender light swirls through you edged in the brilliant white light of God, know you are one with the God energy and you are whole. Accept it all, filling every part of your body, heart, mind and spirit with the divinity that is yours now.

The color of lavender assists in connecting you with your Creator, and in this space of eternal love and power you are guided into acceptance of all that is. It was the first celestial color given for this healing advancement. It is of utmost importance that any being who desires healing in any dimension begin with their connection to their Creator. There is no other way to begin but at the beginning, and the beginning and end of everything in the universe, including you, is God. And so it is in this space that the angels began their masterpiece.

No matter the challenge you are experiencing, you are greater than it is. Through this color you can feel your oneness with all that is noble and worthy, with the Healer of the universe, and here you can appreciate the fullness of gratitude for your present life experience. Imagine beautiful spun silk, its texture flowing graciously against your body in luxurious harmony. Here abides amazing peace. Peace is born of love which accepts divine perfection in all things. Love heals.

The amethyst, in multiple hues of purple to lavender shades, is a stone that reveals healing energy from the eons of time. It is healing for the mind, heart, body and spirit. Holding it enables you to be deeply connected to the universal vibration of love, which is the essence of all healing power. It allows through its frequencies to transmute into higher spiritual and ethereal levels of knowingness. It is a conduit for the energy of calm and peacefulness.

In your mind's eye, lift a sparkling amethyst into the palm of your hand, feeling the calm reaching deep into your soul. Feel your mind, heart, body and spirit aligning with the pure love and light of the universe while healing surges through your entire being. See your spirit being lifted into higher realms of alignment with who you really are. Know your power and perfection and feel that perfection permeating all areas that need healing within you.

And so it is…

From:

Hope

Your power lies in the endless source of your Creator.

All you need is to accept it.

Macindea

The Angel of Pink

Velvety softness following the flow of
lavender and oneness with God,
a vision of love spreading throughout
opening our heart to its core.
Stretching and giving, moving beyond,
erasing the pain and dismay,
it is love that appreciates all that you are
and honors the purity of truth.

Precious Macindea, Angel of Love,
opening our hearts to remember.

Chapter 2

Second Light: Pink

Gem: Rose Quartz

Flower: Pink Rose

Feeling:
Appreciation

*A*s the lavender fades away, turn your attention to the celestial color of pink, soft and fuzzy, giving meaning to the sense of appreciation. Gracefully descending, spiraling and swirling, it expands in the appreciation of life itself. Dispelling disorder it moves through chaos with ease, opening up the chambers so long abandoned for lack of love. As the love sweeps in, fineness spreads throughout.

Pink is the eye of the heart. The heart cannot see without love, and only the frequency created by the vibrations of love can ever open you to your realness. The pink softens the rough edges melting away discord, hurt, doubts and fears of all description just as snow melts when the sun's rays shine through on a cold winter day.

Love expands the heart into new dimensions of expression and possibilities. It opens the doors of compassion so that enemies become friends and beings in pain can feel vibrations of hope embracing them. Compassion reaches out to touch hearts that may otherwise never be touched, and it is only from love that such is expressed.

Imagine right now a fluffy ball of cotton candy or the soft, twitching nose of a cuddly rabbit. See a bouquet of velvety pink roses beckoning for you to touch their soft petals, or pink ribbons adorning the bouncing curls of a sweet little girl. You notice how you feel as you imagine these things, how they make you warm while you smile in the fullness of love.

See the pink love traveling throughout any disorder within your being, dissipating it completely as it passes through. Notice the shift within you, the lightness as you let go of the old and invite in the new. This shift opens you for healing as you stretch beyond what you believed before was true. All judgment leaves your premises and is replaced with understanding and appreciation.

Open your nostrils to the aroma of the roses, spectacular in their beauty. They give rise to a feeling of nobility as they open their petals to welcome you. Add to that aroma the wonderful fragrance of a camellia with bright shiny leaves that sparkle in the dancing sunlight.

Pink opens the heart to honor its purity. In the state of purity one can see the Self as it truly is, one that is born of love and is always seeking to reconnect to that same place of love. Here there is truth, and truth allows for the appreciation of all things. It is in a space of love that one can appreciate any ailment or challenge as a gift from God. Once it is appreciated and accepted as part of the truth, healing can begin.

So now, look deep into your being at the challenges presently around you. Know with me that this is a gift, for without this gift how would you see? You have been given a powerful opportunity to expand beyond what you presently see and become more, more of truth, more of love, and therefore more of spirit. See the blessings and say "Thank you God." Feel your heart awakening with those thoughts of appreciation, expanding the pink love past your heart space into greater depths within your being. Feel it pulse through your entire body, encircling you both inside and out. You may feel tears. Let them flow for you are truly melting away all that does not serve your highest good. Honor this place and see the intention of your true vision.

Now focus your thoughts into your heart space. In your mind's eye imagine you are holding in your hand a magnificent specimen of rose quartz. Feel the great warmth it dispels outward into your hand. As the light of love radiating from your heart hits the stone's facets, a brilliant display of glittering rays swirl throughout your being, overflowing the feeling of love into every nook and cranny of your total being until you overflow beyond your present body cover. An amazing sense of appreciation of your own Self overtakes your awareness as you glow with divine love. Know that what you are presently feeling can be brought into your awareness at any given moment, for it never leaves your heart. Simply go deep within and align with this feeling and the flow begins. It cannot be stopped unless you choose to stop it.

In this space of acceptance and appreciation of you and whatever is presently in your life experience, you are healing. Now you are ready for the next celestial color and its feeling.

And so it is...

From:

Macindea

Open your heart to divine love, for love is all there is.

Angelique

The Angel of Green

Surrender, release, for it is time
to erase the old that is tattered and torn,
for it covers not nor warms our heart
so left behind it must be.
Drawing in the freshness of spring
a time of rebirth to allow the new,
clearing away to uncover the vibrancy
of all that is.

We welcome you Angelique
as you light the way for us to flourish.

Chapter 3

Third Light: Green

Gem: Peridot

Flower: Angelica

Feeling:
Surrender

*L*ike a mist on a foggy day, the celestial green flows into your awareness now. It covers the outside and gradually seeps within your being. It brings a powerful force to sweep away the debris that has been cluttering your path, assisting you in a major spring cleaning, so that you can surrender the old to make way for the new.

It's as if tiny whisk brooms are released and begin brushing and scrubbing their way through the clutter, going into every passageway and clearing things away. See the angels whisking out the rubbish, placing it in piles to be swept into the depths of mother earth or carried off into the wind forever. It is clearing the cobwebs of doubt, fear, pain and hurt. As the cleaning continues, fresh surfaces are revealed, and with that there is a feeling of rebirth.

Smell the freshness of cool mint as it opens the nostrils to breathe once again. Picture an entire field of mint as the aroma perfumes the hillside. Imagine freshly squeezed limes adding tartness upon your lips. Smell the breeze that lifts your spirit after a newly fallen rain.

Touch with your mind your inner Self and feel the purifying as if it is hung out to dance in the gentle breeze like sheets drying on the clothesline on a warm spring afternoon. Crisp, fresh and renewed, the regeneration of something stale and soiled can happen as you allow the flow of heaven's divine breath. Cleaning out all that no longer serves your highest good allows for perfect symmetry in the flow of all that you deserve. Releasing and sweeping away the old patterns make it possible to bring into your reality what you truly want and deserve, even the healing of your body, your heart, or your spirit.

In this moment, see what needs to be cleared out in order for wholeness to return to you. It is your birthright and you can claim it now. See the pain, the illness, the sadness, the worry, the struggle, whatever blocks your life from wholeness. Watch it float away with the stream's current that reaches to the center of the earth where it is released into its ending. Feel the weight of it leave you as you allow your spirit to be lifted up and restored. Accept the purity of the soft green light that now surrounds you, in and throughout your being. It is your knowingness that can bring this freshness into your soul so that you are revived completely.

Surrender to your creator all that is not worthy of you. It is in the surrender that you become powerful and have the knowingness of wholeness and the power to make it appear for you. Place that knowingness deep into your being so that you can be restored to the original state of your essence from which you came. All is possible and you can make it so. Now see the soft green power floating in and out through you, and allow the healing of all that is not perfect to ensue.

At this moment, see and feel the dew on vibrating green leaves of the forest. It sparkles as the sun's rays befall it, glistening like brightly colored gems. All is alive and thriving and as you connect to that energy of the brightly colored gems, you are validating your spirit's power to refresh you. It is in this space that you become the powerful being you already are and can add vibrancy to not only yourself but all those who cross your path.

The soft celestial green depicts growth and movement. Here your energies can be balanced and expand into new realms of awareness as you grow beyond anything you previously thought imaginable. It can stimulate greater awareness of nature which possesses all of life and its answers.

Consider Angelica, a flower of the earth, used for its healing capabilities. Its stalks are tall with clusters of greenish flowers. The roots and fruit are used to bathe the souls of those with maladies while others use them for flavorings. It is a feminine flower, derived appropriately from your word angelic.

Now take into your mind's eye the peridot crystal. Feel the warm and friendly energy that is emitted from the inner recesses of this stone. It can assist in a further understanding of all that is transpiring while helping to uncover and cast aside the detrimental patterns that have so longed plagued your heart, soul and body. The tonic-like abilities of this stone both strengthen and regenerate the body while providing an enlightened state in your healing. Focusing on this stone can offer a shield of protection from outside negative influences. Feel its power as you bring it within you. Surrender to it.

And so it is…

From:

Angelique

Allow the angels to help you release the old

so you can be renewed.

Jasmine

The Angel of Yellow

Like a touch of sunshine
warming the heart and making if glow,
surging through as a current of light
that brightens even the darkest path.
Smiling on every being
who wishes to bask in all its glory,
softening the dry crusty edges of pain
as healing creeps silently within and without.

You are indeed welcome dear Jasmine,
wafting in with the light of love.

Chapter 4

Fourth Light: Yellow

Gem: Citrine

Flower: Daffodil

Feeling:
Nourishing

*I*nvite in the glowing celestial color of yellow, wafting in like a mist of rapturous light, the beams filtering in as if through prisms of sunlight. It warms the hearts of all who see and feel it, bringing a smile to the lips of even the sad and lonely. Like a soft, fuzzy blanket it wraps around your being, caressing you with the touch of healing that penetrates the soul.

It is as if the Light of God winks at you, spreading its glory about you, softening the roughness with divine love. Pain melts away as does worry, for when the sun shines people shed their frowns and create a happy face. Cozy and relaxed, one snuggles down into the depths of this radiating warmth, like the serenity of a fire glowing in the fireplace on a cold winter's night.

This light of golden yellow nourishes the heart and soul with the good you deserve, spreading throughout, casting its shadow as the afternoon sun. Lying on the beach, wiggling your toes through the heated sand, laughing with glee as children who delight in the excitement of life, 'tis the miracle of this light. Crusty edges melt away from shadowing the heart's true beauty so that the Light of God can smile into all crevices and corners, healing all that is not of love.

Taste the lemon, tart in its own right, cleansing and pure. Breathe deeply and smell the lusciousness of the fragrant honeysuckle blossoms that permeate the air around them, sweet and inviting. Pick a delicate blossom and watch as nectar slips quietly from its stem. Hear the beautiful song of the canary, a brilliant display of bright yellow feathers, small yet strong. Reach out with your mind and gently touch the yellow buttercup as it nods its head in approval of the gift of nature.

A field of daisies invites you to walk with feet bare between the flowers in all their majesty. Their smiling faces, yellow framed with white, beckon you to take a few home to enjoy for tomorrow. Little girls, dancing through the fields, golden hair blowing as their straw bonnets have fallen over their shoulders. No worries are here, carefree as a kite flying that dips and soars with each gust of wind. It is easy to be in the space of this light where all is perfect and flowing in harmony.

Having purged all that is no longer needed, the warmth of this yellow can easily filter its rays into all areas that await its healing beams. Focus your thoughts with this warmth and feel it steal slowly over every part of you that wants to be whole. Pull it in, allowing it to soak into every corner, melting away anything that lingers but no longer serves your highest good. Feel the expansion with this miraculous internal fire as it replenishes below and above, in and throughout, over and around.

With your mind's eye, glance to the heavens and see the host of angelic cherubims dancing on clouds, Their smiles light up the sky and their laughter brings joy to all who see. Garments of celestial yellow flow behind them. They appear to be watching you, waiting for the moment. In a twinkling of an eye, as if rehearsed to perfection, they raise their wings, bowing them forward, and grace you with beautiful angel dust that sprinkles down silently as snow flakes would drift down in the silence of a winter night, blanketing the earth.

Behold the daffodil, resplendent in varying shades of yellow, white and gold. Its form is as a trumpet which heralds the coming of a new beginning. Imagine a host of angelic beings resounding with perfection as they lift their heavenly instruments in harmonious brilliance, acknowledging the rebirth within you.

Yellow is the color of the solar plexus, the charka in the middle of the body that converges the upper chakras with the lower ones. It is here that all aspects of life are digested, but if the energy is blocked then the assimilation of the spiritual truths become overrun with the fear-driven aspects that exist in this life experience. By focusing on the glowing soft yellow one can reopen the energy channel so that there is once again balance which precipitates the digestion of all that is truth. Understanding what is truth allows for the awakening of all that is possible.

Through your mind's eye, place into your hand the quartz stone citrine. This particular mineral does not accumulate negative energy so never needs to be cleared. As you feel this stone in your hand, notice how it warms and energizes, for that is one of its great gifts. It stimulates both the physical body and the mental forces, enhancing the flow of energy and creating more endurance for these realms. It is a marvelous aid for soothing, relaxing, promoting inner radiance and for brightening even the darkest remote corner of an individual's reality. At the same time it generates a flow of courage and inner strength to move through whatever fear ensnares a being.

Like a touch of the smiling rays of sunshine, allow this softly glowing celestial yellow light encased by brilliant white light to penetrate the deepest recesses of your being and feel the power of this light, connected to the One Source, spread the healing force in and through you now, replenishing your soul.

And so it is…

From:

Jasmine

Feel the light that warms the heart,

softening and healing deep within.

Azura

The Angel of Blue

As in the vastness of the endless sky
one can see beyond to all that is possible.
No limits abound unless we create them
for a bigger picture is already in place.
The spaciousness of all that is
opens our eyes to a depth of clarity
bringing to our hearts and souls
the remembrance of who we are.

Expanding and opening into being more,
we greet you Azura with open arms.

Chapter 5

Fifth Light: Blue

Gem: Blue Lace Agate

Flower: Pansy

Feeling:
Spaciousness

*D*escending upon you now is a dreamy celestial blue that brings to mind the sky that has no end. You believe there is an end, but as you approach what you thought was an ending, you realize the sky continues on and on for eternity. This creates a space of unending, and this same space of endlessness is as you are.

In this space of endlessness there are no limits of any description. Everything is a possibility and only in this place of endlessness is the creation of all desires. When limiting conditioning falls away, your eyes become clear so that you see beyond what you thought possible, thus seeing more. The depth perception that accompanies this celestial blue awakens your consciousness into greater spiritual understanding of all that is and all that can be.

Using your imagination, an inborn gift, observe the cosmic forces weaving in and out. Feel the greatness that exists in every realm of your being. Imagination, as if a magic carpet, can take you into the unknown with the speed of lightening and the exhilaration of an adventurous journey. Here you can survey the view of all you can be, and it is here that you can become what you see. The spaciousness allows you to expand more than any way before so that you see beyond the illusion of limitations. This is of great depth and here the richness of the universe is displayed.

Picture the sea, vast and powerful, that flows to the far corners of the earth, connecting all that is. It seems endless as does the sky, and although they appear to meet on the horizon, they never do. Each goes on and on without the other, but both are totally connected through the same spaciousness and universal power. A picture such as this is profound in all its implications, for the endlessness of each gives rise to your own endlessness.

Blue relaxes the mind so it is restful. It cools the overactive energies that spin you into chaos, allowing the respite for which your soul yearns. It presents the calm before the burst of new energy explodes, giving much clarity through that restfulness. One watches the serenity of the sea, sun glistening on the calm waters, knowing that soon, as the tide comes in, the waters will give way to tumultuous waves crashing over the land. There is beauty in all, whether serene or restless, but in the moment of serenity you feel the presence of the Divine Light. In the quietness you can know your essence as one with the Divine Light.

Cool and serene you notice dear Azura standing before you now. This presence filters the blue light through all particles and fields of energy. It's as if the world has calmed, taking a deep breath in, and slowly coming to that place of understanding that the order of the universe is perfect and they are part of that perfection. As if with a magic wand, Azura's light energy sweeps over you and transforms the limitations into all that is possible.

Feel the cool sensation of a mountain stream as it washes over your feet. It is revitalizing at that moment and allows a surge of new energy to pulsate through you. You can now look to the horizon and see the barriers lift as new and exciting possibilities are revealed to you. Glance beyond the stream and notice the wildflowers nodding their heads to you. The violets are nestled in the grassy areas near the stream.

In your mind's eye glance behind you and notice the clusters of pansies in varying shades of blue, lifting their wide-eyed faces as they smile at you. Velvety smooth are their petals. They look at you as if they are saying, "You can do it. Go for it. We are supporting you." Their name means "Heartsease" which is interpreted as peace of mind or calmness of emotion. Seeing the pansy can remind you that you can be peaceful no matter where you are or what is going on around you.

Place in your hand the blue lace agate gem. Feel the depth of spiritual connection with this crystal for it is effective with inner attunement. Feel yourself connect to that higher plane right now. It has been known to enhance one who is seeking extremely high spiritual spaces through balancing the energy of the crown, third eye, throat and heart chakras. This crystal assists when grounding is necessary or in going back to the beginning. It lends itself to gentleness and calm as one might gaze at the beautiful peacefulness in the pale blue sky of endlessness. Individuals with arthritic conditions or those needing healing in their skeletal structure have felt its healing power.

Tune into your own inner depth of connection. Pull the energy of spaciousness into your being and allow the pulsing of this energy to uplift you into higher awareness of your spirit. Extend where you have been before and allow the higher vibrations of possibilities beyond your imagination to drift into your being. See them, feel them, and know they are your truth.

And so it is...

From:

Azura

Gaze into the horizon and see it is endless.
In this spaciousness you are given unending possibilities
and unlimited imagination.

Harmonee

The Angel of Peach

All is well, no disarray,

the gentle breeze barely stirring,

breathing in life's serenity,

feeling sweetness with each breath.

The waves gently cresting

almost silently breaking,

'tis but a moment in time,

and the moment is divine perfection.

With honor we salute you Harmonee

for you bring the tranquility we do seek.

Chapter 6

Sixth Light: Peach

Gem: Pecos Diamond

Flower: Hibiscus

Feeling:
Contentment

$\mathcal{S}$ee the soft celestial hue of peach drifting ever so gently into your view. The sweetness of this color precedes its appearance for it spreads a veil of opulence over you, pulsing through all matter and all space.

Just as gentle ocean breezes waft through the air and into your soul, so does the contentment of soft peach waft into the depths of your beingness.

In this space is oneness with all that is, the space of complete connection with all living things. There is an inner knowing of pure serenity, that all is okay just as it is. We call this divine perfection in a consciousness that reaches the cosmic order of total harmony. It's as if a sweater of warmth is wrapped around you in which you feel comfortable and complete, sinking slowly into the softness of a down comforter that enwraps you. The texture of this color is that of completeness, of soft warmth wrapped around and encompassing body, heart and soul.

Imagine that oneness and how it is all fitting together completely. In your mind's eye see the kid gloves slide easily over the hand in a perfect fit. Watch the hummingbird as it flutters nearby drinking the nectar left for it. That too is a perfect fit. Behold the seashells lingering amongst the sand that line the beach's shores, a perfect match. Now take a moment to relish in the freshness and perfection of a bowl of just picked sliced peaches that appear to swim in the freshly made cream. Listen to the magnificent chorus of voices as they blend together in pleasing perfection. Each one compliments the other and makes it more complete although each part is complete without the other.

The flow of peach is smooth and velvety to the touch. The sound is like musical overtones that blend in a harmonious symphony. Different shapes, sizes, textures, smells, all fitting together in congruent symmetry, each proportionate to the other. We wish your life to be as this, all flowing together in perfect symmetry, all parts as is but together enriching the whole of you. This celestial peach brings to you the musical symphony of life. You see this musical symphony as well as feel it in nature for all goodness is found there. Breathe it in through your nostrils into the center of your being. You are whole if you allow it to be so.

Harmonee's presence is blessing you as you spread the essence of contentment and inner radiance. This presence helps you to see how the trivialities of your life experience are meaningless and only block you from realness. With this presence around you it is possible to understand how easily one can fit with another in complete harmony, and for this you will be grateful.

This softer shade of orange shares joy and wisdom and stimulates the feeling of sociability, all fitting together, interacting one with the other. It lifts the mood and can re-vitalize the spirit and heart as well as the body. Those with emotional paralysis can utilize this soft peach to open to the feelings that benefit the heart and soul, known as love.

See now the beautiful hibiscus flower, nobly calling to you with its beauty. Bell-shaped and magnificent, it beckons to you to hear its melody, as if it is ringing in a new you. Vibrant in the rich shades of peach, coral, rose, golden yellow and white it stands tall and serene, displaying this harmonious blend as a compliment to nature. Its stamens of brilliant yellow hold attraction for the bees which turn it into succulent honey that nourishes and heals.

Feel in your hand the precious stone pecos diamond, a rose-type quartz crystal in its shade of light peach. Its formation creates aggregates of crystals with a multiple range of illumination. This stone has a pleasant air around it and brings joy to the beholder. It balances the chakras, particularly connecting the three lower chakras with the crown chakra. It is a stabilizer of emotions, thus assisting in serenity that brings to you creativity and the knowing of many possibilities.

All is as it is to be. All is divinely orchestrated in perfect harmony. And so you have transcended into the ethereal plane of knowingness for you now have an understanding for creating wholeness within your own being. It takes no effort for the reality is faith - faith in your Creator, faith in your power as co-creator, faith in your essence of divine love, and faith that you came from perfect wholeness and can be that perfect state.

So now relax in the knowingness that all things are taken into consideration and nothing is whirling elsewhere without divine order. Your life is being perfectly orchestrated, and you, with your Creator, have the power to make it exactly what you desire. Create it dear one as you see fit.

And so it is...

From:

Harmonee

Pull into your being the feeling of contentment

and complete your wholeness.

This concludes the advancement that pertains solely to your wholeness. Through these six celestial lights and their feelings, you have the knowingness and the power to become whole right now.

⸎

We now move into elsewhere's of thought, a place in which you project your wholeness for the benefit of other beings. For in the giving you receive, and in the receiving you allow a blessing from and to another. In this gracious state of giving and receiving, you receive many times more than you give. The power comes in the gift of love, and true giving is only from love. There are no expectations in this space.

Join us now as we travel through the place of giving love that is based in your own foundation of love and power. As you give healing love to others, you heal through new realms of awareness, which enraptures your spirit in ecstasy. You grow beyond your own self, connecting to all beings. As you love yourself, you are able to send that love outward, and the celestial colors of healing love are brilliantly intensified through your being and the lives of many others.

Arielle

The Angel of Purple

Like a lion you stand,
strong and powerful,
as a King stands majestically
accepting the power thusly bestowed.
Not with pompous arrogance
but in truth and honor
and the humility that accompanies
from a heart born of love's essence.

In humility we accept the power
and strength you give us Arielle.

Chapter 7

Seventh Light: Purple

Gem: Sugilite

Flower: Iris

Feeling: Magnificence

*F*loating magnificently into your mind's view is the richness of the celestial light purple. Its very presence signifies a majestic flow of energy and power. It bears credence to kings and royalty as well as your Higher Power. Just as a lion rules over the animal kingdom in quiet regality, so do those who reflect the connectiveness to the Higher Power from within their being.

Purple states the divine power of truth, and when you stand for truth and listen to your inner guidance of truth, you are powerful beyond comprehension. In this space there is a deeper dimension of endless possibilities that continually shower you with noble opportunities. As you draw on those opportunities and create more of the same, you enable others to do likewise. Your power is reflective with the vibrations of those who enter your life path which resonates with your higher vibrations.

Never in history has the world been able to open to possibilities as it is right now. The angels are stirring people into awareness that there is more. Souls cry out for more depth and meaning to all aspects of their life. When one understands their own truth and power and adheres to it, then, and only then, can they guide others into a broader spectrum of what really is. This is the enlightenment that enfolds you and enables you to assist others on their journey. Although each individual bears their own truth, the power of those who stand in their power and truth can propel others into potential awareness of who they are and can be.

The celestial light of purple suggests the magnificence of every being ever created. Utilizing this color is a reminder that in accepting all that is as perfection and allowing inborn magnificence to emerge, a like feeling is radiated to those you meet. They in turn are able to see the hope for personal magnificence within the realm of their beingness. The feeling that emits from within you is not something that must be contrived or prepared, it simply flows forth with complete freedom in its magnetic direction. As you touch the magnificence you raise up tall as a champion who is receiving his acclaim.

The softer hue of this celestial color that filtrated your being as the First Light of Lavender signified the feeling of acceptance, acceptance of you just as you are but going deeper into knowing your soul so that resistance departs from within you. In this awareness you can reverently radiate to others the feeling of their own magnificence, for as you accept yourself and stand in awe of your magnificence, you can reflect this powerful, divine energy of magnificence into the aura of those who are ready to accept it. You have become a guide for others to follow as your light is available to guide them through their darkness.

As your mind remembers the mountains that towered before you in glorious splendor as you allowed the soft lavender to penetrate your being, see the same mountains displayed in their glory and power for the benefit of those who await in readiness. Every manifestation is available for all in the same moment as each of us is part of the whole body of energy. The symmetry of vibrations allows for this to be.

The Iris, indeed of noble creation, stands tall for the world to view. Its flowers, though delicate, offer great beauty with the majestic rainbow of lavender and purple hues as their sword-shaped leaves give credence to that of protection. Iris means messenger of the gods and the flowers themselves appear in trios composed of three petals and three drooping sepals.

Focus your mind's eye to the crystallized mass called sugilite, a South African mineral. Its hue of color ranges from violet to purple and has a powerful healing enactment. It represents the perfection of spiritual love and the knowing for all that is. As it assists in the opening of passageways through the various chakras, it provides a pathway for the movement of powerful divine energy. Meditation is measurably enhanced if sugilite is applied, with magical revelations of spiritual understanding. As the mountains viewed within this color show power, incorporating sugilite into the view adds the feeling of being free, perhaps standing atop the majestic mountains with the breeze rippling through one's hair. This same freedom and the powerful feeling of soaring to unknown heights of all possibilities, is revealed to you and those attracted to you by magnetic centricity.

Thrones and Principalities, divine angelic beings of the highest power, remain omnipresent to those who seek a higher element of cosmic force. Call on them to assist in overcoming great resistance to the divine flow of perfection and love. Moving through the resistance to your own power allows for the spreading of truth to others. Rising to a higher level of spiritual awareness is your soul's mission in your life experience, and by calling on the highest powers to assist you throughout, you open the channels for great leaps into your true divine essence from which you came. In so doing you enable your strength to explode into the force known to you before you accepted your present physical form, which enables you to support those who come to you for guidance.

Accept your magnificence as part of your being. Know it intrinsically for it showers you with gems that sparkle magically into higher remembrance of all that is and all that you are. As it resonates within you, it can resonate outwith you.

And so it is…

Arielle

Remember the magnificence of your birth,

arising from the line of divine nobility.

Megalo

The Angel of Rose

Strong and vibrant you do shine

emitting rays of love,

a power that pulsates within and without

as a golden sphere of light.

Balancing and stabilizing,

providing attunement to the higher self,

connecting the energies throughout

so they can be radiated outwith.

Dearest Megalo, we treasure the

feeling of magnetism you give us.

Chapter 8

Eighth Light: Rose

Gem: Rhodochrosite

Flower: Azalea

Feeling:
Magnetism

*F*eel and see coming through you now the elegance and warmth of the celestial light rose, its beams radiating out beyond what you can envision. Feel the surgence of love swirl around and through your entire being creating such a rush of pulsating divine energy that you feel weighted to the earth. Know this is the undeniable power of a great divine love within you, enabling you to project this warmth and power to the world.

In this place you are aware of your inner strength, as a rock on which much can be supported. This strength reflects the foundation of the divine world from whence you came and continues to shower upon you and those who allow. It is as if your heart has expanded into an unending periphery of love, pulsating throughout the energy fields surrounding you and all other beings. Streams of light boomerang outward from within you and continually find their way back to you, as a magnet draws unto itself.

Observe a mother's love, exhibiting an eternal cord that connects her and her child in a never-ending bond. You see that strength, but know that the cord of power that connects you with the love from whence you came is beyond what you can comprehend, its strength far exceeding a mother's love, for it is the strongest power in the universe. It glows outward with a magnetic charisma when expressed from within a being of love. This is your mission: to spread this love as a bearer of it. As it is within, it can be given outwith.

All who are in the world seek love, but most do not understand its meaning. They think it is to fill a void within them, yet no being or thing can ever fill that void. Humans seek validation from their external world and they believe that validation is love. Love is born within so nothing in your world can ever fill that space of love. Although there is much good in your world that gives you pleasant feelings and you interpret as love, it is not love. Love is of the heart, deep within, where you are connected by the divine cord of light to your Creator. Only there is love found, and only there can love be expressed and freely given. In this space you are real.

Love has no bindings, no needs, and no demands. Love simply is. Nothing is stronger than this pure love that bears no attachment. Love is always free, and in that freedom is the power of love. So freely give your love to every being and creature in your world. Love heals, expands and warms the heart of everyone. Love overrules the power of fear, for love is indeed many times stronger. The world can receive great credence from this love at this time as there is much born from fear. Beings lie in wait for the expressions of fear, expecting them to come, so they appear. Instead, dear one, pour love from your heart so that it reaches the far corners of the world and warms the frozen hearts until they melt, dissolving the fears.

Love allows for balance. When fear prevails the scales are not equal, for the heaviness pulls it down. But love brings back the balance. The equilibrium of balance gives rise to a constant flow of love that can transcend all depths of despair and create healing for the world. This is what we give to you: the power of love to create balance in the world, something for which the world hungers.

Behold the clusters of rose colored flowers of the azalea. Its beauty unfolds as it heralds in the first of spring following the starkness of winter. It sprinkles in brilliant array the gardens of your planet, displaying in breathtaking beauty the mysteries of the universe. As the azalea bursts into the beauty of spring after the dormancy of winter, so does love infiltrate the deepest recesses of the heart that has been closed with the fears that haunt each being who has allowed them in.

In your mind's eye reach for the rose crystal named rhodochrosite. You can feel the pulsating electrical energy of this stone of love and balance. It is filled with a golden sphere of light as the divine energies pulsate through it. The energy of this stone helps you in your service to the planet and allows you to feel joy in this responsibility. It has been known to enhance the release of dysfunctional negative aspects and aid in strengthening intestinal tract, heart and thyroid imbalances.

Remember that you are likened to a magnet, for this you are indeed. Your presence gives vibrating beams that tells the world your inner composition. Take heed that you hold only love within for whatever is within you is what you share with others.

And so it is...

Megalo

Like a magnet the love within you

can change the world, one at a time.

Samantha

The Angel of Jade Green

Wearing strength and fortitude you come

in remembrance of the power within,

creating the life stream of all creativity

for the inner joyousness it can bring.

Cool and serene, not a flicker of the eye,

standing steadfast amongst the hurdles of life,

seeing the brilliance, the sparkle of newness,

the regeneration like each drop of dew.

In appreciation for your sign of strength and

power, we accept your gift dear Samantha.

Chapter 9

Ninth Light: Jade Green

Gem: Jade

Flower: Forest Foliage

Feeling:
Regeneration

*F*irmly yet gently feel the celestial color of jade green enter your being adding great strength and energy to you now. Feel yourself being lifted up with renewed courage and life. Know that this is your birthright power and it is simply renewing in you what is already yours.

As the energy surges through your body and soul, realize the regeneration that is taking place at this moment. Pulsing in every direction throughout you is a powerful creative spirit of healing energy, an energy that pulses through every being on the planet. When coming from the power of fortitude, there is a patient endurance that allows any individual to become all they can be, going beyond all conceivable interpretations of what is. Everything is possible so that with this burst of fortitude and courage you are able to give amazing love to those within your field of vibrations.

Behold the brilliance of life for it is right before your eyes. Many shield their eyes from this light for fear it may blind them, but it does not. Instead it can lead you into a greater awareness of yourself and others as it transcends the knowledge of earth. Allow this awareness to open into fullness and flow into your being. This is the place of greatness where all seeds of creativity are planted, waiting for the birth of all new things. So is the law of the universe unfolding for you: the seed is planted, it is nourished and fed, and becomes a magnificent display of beauty as it bursts into something new and full of vibrant life.

In the process of regeneration, which is the release of the old and the bursting forth of new, there is a space of waiting. Waiting is not liked by most beings so you are being given the understanding of this art, for it is patience and must truly be mastered. All healing and growth requires an allowance of divine timing because this space of waiting builds great foundations of strength and fortitude. In order to assist in the healing of the world it will take the building up of great foundations, strong enough to support the weaker who lean heavily on those who have the strength we are teaching you now.

Glance into the horizon and see wholeness that awaits the planet. It is available for any who believe in this possibility and are willing to build. The name Samantha means prophet, a divinely inspired guide who is a spokesman for the cause of their heart. You are a spokesman for the world, a light that can divinely inspire others because of your brilliance. Your heart's cause is love, for love is all there is.

So glance into the eyes of the world. What do you see? There are tears and sorrows, hostility and wars, sadness and unhappiness, hollow eyes where joy is not seen. There is no love in these eyes for they are looking blindly into the eyes of fear. My dear one, you have the wisdom and the strength to give sight to these eyes for you are love. It must be within you for sharing with the world, and the regeneration that you allowed within is enabling you to give the same outwith. For this you are blessed even though waiting may have been difficult for you. To all things there is reasoning and the faith to persevere is the power that is born of you.

As an example of patience and the enlightenment that was the result, you are able to assist others with their journey of regeneration into wholeness. Go forth and offer a hand to those who are reaching for your hand, but leave the rest to be in their place.

Imagine you are walking through a dense forest, which is overladen with the richness of nature's beauty. All is green around you, the symbol of life itself, of rebirth, of newness, of energy and vitality. Touch the foliage as you walk by and feel its power, springing forth the divine energy that depicts the elixir of life.

There is present great strength and regeneration, for in each season we see changes in the foliage. But no matter what appears on the outside the energy of life is always within. The old falls away, time passes, and the vitally new is revealed once again.

Envision the dream stone of jade, for it is known for its enhancement of dreaming as well as the release of suppressed emotions during the dreaming state. It is known to assist one in the release of their own limitations so that regeneration of their life can unfold. Feel in this stone right now the power it emanates for wholeness, releasing the old and inspiring the surge of new.

In the essence of your being is all the power needed for regeneration in any dimension. We simply ask you to patiently display your birthright strength so you can uphold those who need your strength. Their strength can then develop until they too can uphold another.

And so it is...

Samantha

Accept the time and space for regeneration of the soul,

for it indeed does come.

Magical and illuminating

the divine light of God does shine forth,

radiating its beams to the world

so the world can see.

Warming and giving

the heart of gold reaches out,

expanding and uplifting

each soul one at a time.

Blessed are we with your presence dearest Starr

for you bring the glorious light of love.

Chapter 10

Tenth Light: Golden Yellow

Gem: Topaz

Flower: Buttercup

*F*eel the warmth of the celestial golden yellow that appears in your horizon now. It bears a brilliant glow that illumines the sky. Behold the prisms that radiate outward through this brilliance, for surely the energy of God is in this light.

That is the feeling of this celestial light, the feeling of total illumination. It is the feeling that comes from within a being of love when only the radiating energy of love comes forthwith from this being. It dazzles the world so to speak with its illuminating power as it lights up the darkness.

As you pull the golden yellow through your being, feel the flow of warmth that transpires. It literally penetrates to the depth of your soul, for that is the nature of love. As in its softer shaded color, this celestial yellow melts away all that is born of fear. The crusty edges of doubt, self-incrimination, anger and malice slowly ebb away, as a tide that washes away the debris left on the sands of the beach. Feel the golden yellow submerge your soul into the depth of love as you've never before experienced right now, knowing that when you surface your heart will be generating the love of God if you allow it in. At that moment of allowing you become the instrument you were meant to be, an instrument that radiates the love of God for all to see.

Focus on the golden ball of energy you call the sun. To gaze at it brings tears to your eyes for its brilliance. That is the power you have as an instrument of God with the ability to bring tears that wash away the fears so love can emerge. That is the power of illumination – the power to give out what dwells within your being. This is possible when you accept the love of God and allow it to expand into the world. This is your calling. Only now, as it is within you, can it be displayed for the planet, for it is only possible to give what dwells within your heart. It is your responsibility to display the love of God and this is the source of your healing power. The celestial yellow, in both shades, is the light of healing in all dimensions of beingness.

See in your minds view the friendly, happy buttercup. It seems to speak to you of sweetness as we think upon sweet butter. To hold the buttercup under your chin there is a glowing reflection of yellow that makes one smile. That is the nature of this flower—to make you smile.

Such is the nature of the light of God—to make you smile. Does not warmth from the sun that melts away the coldness of a winter day make you smile? Is not your spirit lifted when the sun peeks from behind a dark layer of clouds?

We ask you to pass along a smile in all days of your life. Your smile will warm the hearts of many and in turn can make them smile. This can continue forward until the entire world is smiling, just because you gave the first smile. Your inner smile is possible because of the love that resides within you. We've told you this many times but humans forget so it must be repeated. Love creates a smiling face and this is a gift to all who see you.

Take into consideration the beautiful topaz stone. Topaz acts as an energy conductor that relays a message outwith. The message within is radiated through vibrations and is repeated as is. This energy transcends both time and space and creates an ethereal magnetic effect. It is powerful as a means of enhancing all healing, whether of body, mind or spirit. Hold it in your hand and feel the surge of healing power that already resides in your soul.

We cannot speak to you enough about your divine mission of spreading the essence of love. It is your heritage and the heritage of all around you, but all do not know. Thus is your mission on earth: To spread the love of God to all the world, for nothing is greater than this. In sharing this love you raise your own spirit into higher realms of awareness and depth of life experiences. The only thing that matters in your world or any world is love, regardless of anything that ever was conceived in your thoughts aforehand.

Now go dear one and illumine the world with the love that radiates from your soul and the heart of God. Expand this love into the heart of the world, for such is your glory.

And so it is…

From:

Starr

Your mission on this planet is to illuminate the world

with the love in your heart.

Victor

The Angel of Vibrant Blue

Bringing to us courage and amazing valor

to step into the unknown,

to take the risk no matter what

which a heart filled with love can do.

Forever expanding above and beyond

the horizon continually rising,

moving outward, lifting your eyes

to see more than was imagined afore.

We are blessed with your fearlessness

and the courage you bring dear Victor.

Chapter 11

Eleventh Light: Vibrant Blue

Gem: Lapis Lazuli

Flower: Hydrangea

Feeling:
Expansion

*B*ehold the beauty of the celestial vibrant blue filtering through the clouds of life as it extends to you a new hunger for more. Pull it into the very essence of your soul and project it forthwith to the ends of the earth. Allow this vitality to spread in massive quantum leaps, touching hearts and changing lives.

Remember the softer shade of celestial blue that opened for you new awareness of all that lies beyond what can be seen. Know that this endlessness that abides within you now awaits the spirits of all beings, but many do not understand this thought. Your regenerated vitality can reflect this intention into all areas of your planet and shake the energy into motion at a faster speed.

Everything perpetuates outward whether in a knowing sense or without guidance. Nothing is random or a happenstance without design, for all is orchestrated from the eternal realm of your origin. Place your thought to the beings of the world and send the much needed love that their heart yearns for, and you will see miracles unfold in all dimensions. All will expand. The angels are stirring hearts for readiness and you are a vessel that is filled to overflowing to bring them new hope and possibilities.

Victor comes to you to offer fearlessness as has not been experienced before. The words have been there within you and others but the knowingness has eluded you. Picture before you a running brook with fresh spring water. Many tell you of its purity and coolness, and in your mind you can envision the concept, but until you drop your feet into the brook or place the water into your hand and put it into your mouth there is not knowingness. Thus it is the experience and the feeling of the experience that allows you to know its purity and coolness. So it is with the fearlessness that Victor offers to you now. To know it means to experience this within your being.

Fearlessness allows individuals to move into uncertain territory with feet planted solidly without a quiver. Their faith is strong and they do not fear this as a risk for they know the power greater than all is connected to them. Therefore only perfection is present in any situation. Stepping out becomes an exciting adventure into higher awareness of all that is when fearlessness abides within your being. Valliant you are when in the space of fearlessness.

Breathe in the braveness that flows with this vibrant blue. Feel it propelled to the depths of your soul as in turn you breathe it outward to those who are ready for it. Although they can receive this courage themselves, many need assistance to know it. As all energy is really one, one being's fearless energy can shift many, for it is a continuous movement, going forth and returning.

Think a moment upon the beautiful hydrangea bush laden with vibrant blue flower clusters. It displays a lushness with large, prolific balls of showy blossoms. It receives its origin from the saxifrage family of bushes. The meaning is rock as these plants can be found growing amongst rocks. This is appropriately named for this celestial color since it requires steadfastness, like a rock, to step out in faith when all is not seen. This is what we are telling you. It is time to know your strength and step out for the world to see and then follow. People will watch and as a leader you can guide others on their journey and help them see more than their mind has ever conceived before. Although it must begin with the thought of the mind, and many have done so, it is the movement that creates the expansion. Each are equally important and you must follow the other in oneness.

The lapis lazuli is a crystal that forms in masses as does the hydrangea blossoms. Its richness is apparent through its shade of vibrant blue. Feel it in your hand right now for it helps an individual expand awareness and intellectual capacity as well as attunes the psychic and intuitive aspects of your being. One of its blessings is its ability to stimulate and awaken your perfect self, and giving more clarity while releasing you from an emotional prison.

Look to your horizon right now and know it extends beyond what you see. Look somewhat deeper and you can see more. As you continue to do this, more will be seen, and as you reach one place, you step beyond it and see another. And so is the journey of expansion for each soul, each one expressing according to their path.

And so it is...

From:

Victor

Allow the movement within the universe to expand

you into new realms of awareness,

for that is the true measure of a soul.

Salome

The Angel of Coral

We see such clarity, an inner knowingness,

allowing for total peace,

for with this angel comes a glow

that inspires from deep within.

Radiating outward for all to see

because it is within,

there is a depth perception that

transcends the knowledge of one afore.

With humility and gratitude we welcome

the glow of life within our soul, opening to

the gift of Salome.

Chapter 12

Twelfth Light: Coral

Gem: Pink Coral

Flower: Zinnia

Feeling: Knowingness

*E*nrapturing you now is the celestial light coral, brilliantly displaying for the world to see the inner glowing for life itself. This glowing for life is deep within your soul as that soul has a knowingness of the universal oneness of all that is. Pull this celestial light into the innermost places of your being and feel that oneness.

For each is a part of the other yet remains individual as is. The cosmic energy that travels around the world allows all to be connected in the one vibration. One being of peace can spread the vibration of peace to all members of the planet, creating then perfect harmony and tranquility.

Knowingness is a deep understanding of divine order, knowing that it isn't necessary to really know anything at all. In this space there is trust that all is in perfection and unfolding at just the right time. There is no worry or anxiety over things that need to be done, for in this space there is faith that all is already taken care of and will manifest in divine timing. In this place is perfect peace.

It is as if a being can lean back in a comfortable chair and relax, for their worries do not produce desired endings—the endings are already decided. When this concept is internalized a being knows with clarity never before known to them. It is simply allowing all that is to manifest for them. It presents to this being an awareness and continuity for the normal ebb and flow of their life.

The feeling of knowingness allows you to envision great possibilities, to see way beyond the normal range of thought. It gives a distinct desire to move forward, like a push from within, knowing there is more. Life has received new energy, a vibrancy that resounds as it moves to and fro with much energetic activity. Thus is the power within you if you allow it to be used.

So as this vibrant energy is released into the world, the magnetism of energy will latch onto other beings who are ready to move forward. It will bring them into the flow of vibrant energy so they too can see beyond all that has been before. Imagination, in its most mystical parameter, is what creates forward movement, for without new dreams of what can be it could not be.

Dear beings, feel the inner tranquility of being present in each moment. In the presence of each moment is the knowingness of all time, all reason, all wisdom, all love. There is no other place but the now moment. Here again is a place of peace, complete serenity, for here you are real and connected to your higher self. As you see the moment, you feel a contentment that goes beyond reason, for in that place of the moment there is only love. Love is your essence dear one, and love is the only thing that is real.

Imagine a piece of coral; hold it in your hand. It will assist you in visualizing with incredible imagination all that can be. It represents concurrence of the universal energies so that the flow of life connects and revives all beings in order for new ideas and inspirations to manifest. It supports the knowledge that everyone and everything within the universe is connected by the eternal bonds of love. This is the knowingness of which we speak. Breathe it in through your nostrils and absorb it within so you in turn can breathe it out for all beings who so need this.

Picture in your mind's eye the beautiful zinnia, strong and sturdy in stem, easily grown in any soil. Such is love: strong and sturdy and easy to be grown at any place. Its flowers dance in colorful array to decorate any garden. Their beauty endures as does the beauty of love and peace.

So now dear beings, see the grand picture of life. Feel the serenity in coming to that place of knowingness, a place where the externals of your life have no bearing on your spirit. Your spirit is your realness and there and there alone is the essence of your being. This place of realness projects outward as glowing embers in a fire, pulling you towards it in subtle mystical magnetism.

Behold, you are free when you allow total peace in regards to the unknown of life. The beauty of it all is that in the unknown lies all the mysteries of life just waiting to unfold. These mysteries are the fire within you that can propel you into the vibrancy for all of life and its many miracles. Come to a place of knowingness dear beings, and there you can be whole. In your wholeness the entire world can too be whole.

And so it is…

From:

Salome

Allow peace and serenity to direct your life

for the unkowns of life bring into form

your amazing imagination.

Dolcei

The Angel of Dove Gray

Like a blanket you do come

to cover the earth with simplicity,

giving the feeling of balance

in the midst of chaos.

Spreading across and around

through disarray so often seen,

combining all into oneness

and sharing the freedom of it all.

We open our hands to accept the gift you bring

of joyful happiness within dear Dolcei.

Chapter 13

Thirteenth Light: Dove Gray

Gem: Hematite

Flower: Gray Santolina

Feeling:
Blissfulness

*F*eel the celestial light of dove gray descending on you now, weaving in and out of your cells, organs, and all systems of your earthly being. Feel this light permeate your soul and heart, giving you the knowing of perfect bliss. As a blanket of snow covers the earth in astonishing beauty, so it is with this light.

As you pull this feeling of bliss throughout you, understand the perfect symmetry of it all, the joining together of all the celestial lights of this advancement as they combine forces into oneness. In this place there is a feeling of heavenly rapture, a sheer ecstasy that catapults the spirit into higher realms of enlightenment and joy. Herein is wholeness.

And so it is in the combination of all, that a magnanimous power emanates through you and outward to the planet. The power is of great strength but its appearance is that of humbleness. For a being of true power does not exemplify it; it simply is. You can feel this power as it radiates from the soul, and you dear one, have this power. It came with you but is often not seen. See it now and allow it to be useful. It is a gift of the spirit.

Flow with the trancelike feeling of spiritual joy that resides within when you are are blissful. Complete serenity abides in that space as it would be when all goes well. You see it is always good, no matter what is being seen, when blissfulness stems from within your being. There is great happiness in this state because nothing in your world can erase it. The things of the world that take up so much space and time for you are here one day and gone the next, and they do not contribute to your great happiness. You may think this is so, but we tell you it is not.

When a being can understand intense delight in all of life and enjoy the participation in the earthly experience, remaining in a constant state of contentment and peace, then this being knows balance. This is important for any life experience for herein lies blissfulness.

There can be a resurgence of your original state for this is how you began, in complete bliss, for when the essence of love from whence you came is in your heart, there can only be contentment. Love cannot reside with the feeling of chaos so focus on your love so it can be spread abroad and about. An even greater joy abides when you share your love with others and you are in that space now. Feel it radiate outward, its beams stretching far beyond what you can see or even feel. What a gift is in this love for it touches the hearts of those who cry out for its touch.

Rest now in the knowing that all around you and within you is in perfect divine order and that even when the wind blows and things seem upturned there is perfect order. It is as the eye of a storm renders peacefulness in that place, so can be your life inside when without produces turmoil. Feel the rapture expressed as great happiness and peace when blissfulness is your life. Imagine how you, in a state of bliss, can calm the souls of many who thrash about in their storm. Blessed are you for this knowingness.

Feel in your hand the woolly texture of the gray santolina. It stands erect as it spreads with ease wherever it is free to grow. Such is this celestial color for it spreads to each corner where it is welcome, in a place where people willingly accept it spreading to them.

Take into your hand the crystal hematite. It stimulates the desire for peace, the desire that resides within all beings, while assisting one in attaining the peace and inner happiness they are seeking. It is conducive to a soft meditative state that brings to one emotional clarity and inner tranquility.

As one opens to the state of blissfulness, one opens to their own power. A person of power can spread that power to another who is open to it with great ease and simplicity, for each is a part of the whole. There is really no mystery in all of this, but simply the absence of remembrance.

Think a moment on the dove, a beautiful winged creature that denotes peace and serenity. Its soft cooing sound is soothing and gentle and is a symbol of the spirit. When you live through your spirit there is peace and your life flows in harmony and gentleness.

Now draw to you as a blanket that warms you from the inside out the celestial dove gray color, wrapping it around and through your being so that the longstanding joy of blissfulness enfolds you, casting the glow of that feeling outward to the world. The world may not be ready to embrace it, yet they will feel the warmth and calm envelope them as a mist that spreads and overtakes without warning. Their mind may not focus unto its meaning, but the heart will feel. It is the feeling of the heart that opens one to peace and love.

And so it is…

From:

Dolcei

In the midst of life's turmoil you have the knowingness

of true bliss. Feel it in your heart beloved beings.

Beloved Ones,

It is our wish that you fully comprehend the meaning of this holy advancement. All power is within you. All of your desires are around you in various ethereal dimensions awaiting your acceptance of them. We wish you no delay in receiving your desires so we give you these messages. Whether your pain is of body, heart, mind or spirit we ask you to simply remember your essence of love and the perfection of your being in all realms of knowingness.

Around you all things move with cosmic force that either raises your vibration or spirals it downward. In raising your thoughts all things are obtainable. If you are seeking physical healing, prosperity, joyous beingness, vitality, loving relationships, serenity, or enrapturing fulfillment, it can be found in every moment that you feel love and give expression of that love.

We implore you to take heed of this so your life can become more of the realness of who you are, giving you treasures of great magnitude in the domain of spiritual enlightenment.

Love, the Angels

And So It Is

These words were given so that you and I, as perfect designs of the Creator, can remember that state of perfection and return to the wholeness of that state. As designs of the Creator of the universe, we are given like energy and power to co-create the same from whence we came. By coming to earth and living in physical form we have forgotten our original essence of love. In accepting a life based on fear we have immersed ourselves in thoughts and behavior contrary to our innate knowing and have often created the opposite of our true desires.

The colors have been given as a reminder of the importance of feeling the love of our origin. None of this is new but has simply been forgotten. In viewing the beauty of nature with our minds and hearts, and the majestic spectrum of color that it perpetuates, we can more easily remember the expression of love that is our real beingness. Feel the colors as they are given, draw them into your being, and restore that which is your birthright—wholeness.

I lived for multiple decades through the eyes of fear, not realizing there was any other way. But as various teachers—people, books, classes, audios—appeared in my life, I opened to the possibility that there is another way to experience life. It has brought me to an amazing place of inner joy, peace and healing of my body, heart, thoughts and spirit. Having dedicated my life as an instrument of service, Divine Infinite Wisdom has channeled through me the messages that I share with you for your highest good and enlightenment. Breathe them in, breathe them out, until they become one with you as it is meant to be. In this space you have the power of the universe to heal and create wholeness within your being.

Carolyn

Abbreviated Visualization of the Six Celestial Lights for Your Healing

Find a quiet place where you will not be disturbed. Close your eyes so as not to be distracted. Take several slow, deep breaths, in through your nose and out through your mouth. Feel your body sinking slowly, relaxing with every breath, your legs and arms feeling weighted down and too heavy to lift.

Now see a brilliant white light surrounding you, bathing you in divine, everlasting love. Feel the wholeness of that light no matter what is going on in your external life. Pull that white light through your crown chakra on the top of your head. It is pure and perfect as you are. Feel that perfection. Direct that light to any area of your being where healing is desired.

Begin now by bringing in the celestial lights one at a time through your crown chakra. See the soft *lavender* spiraling gently into you. Feel the majesty of this color which signifies royalty, knowing you are of that royal lineage. It is as silk that brushes ever so gently against your skin with a lavish richness. *Accept* all that is as good for this is the feeling of lavender, brought to you by the angel Hope. In this place you can be serene as the eye of a storm yields a center of peacefulness amidst turmoil. You are connected to the power of the universe and all things are possible. Accept it all now.

Filtering through you now is *pink*, brought to you by Macindea, its softness opening you to an awareness of your own worth so that you can appreciate you. *Appreciation* is an expression of love, which is your essence, and in this place is the power to erase all that is of lower vibrations that says there is not enough. Inviting in the feeling of appreciation with the color pink can shift you into compassion and understanding for yourself first and then others. The velvety touch of a beautiful pink rose reflects the softness of this feeling as it melts away any rough edges within you.

Allow the celestial *green* to flow through you now. Feel the *release* of all that does not serve your highest good. Allow what you release to flow from you into the center of the earth to be gone from you. Sweep away all old beliefs and understandings of the past and open your heart and soul to the freshness of all that is new. Behold a sprig of mint. Breathe in its fresh aroma and the sense of clean and pure, allowing for perfect symmetry to flow with all that you deserve. This is the gift from Angelique. Release and surrender as you open to the vitality of rebirth and experience vital energy through the sparkling light of this celestial green.

Glowing in front of you is the rapturous light of soft *yellow* as its beams create prisms of beauty around you. Feel the warmth permeate your being like the touch of smiling rays of sunshine as Jasmine gives it to you. Accept the *nourishing* feeling of this yellow as it feeds your being in all dimensions. Its light spreads about you softening the worries and pain in you as a warm cozy fire warms the heart and body on a cold winter's night. Feel the power of this light as it spreads the divine healing force in and through you now.

Look into the vast endlessness of the universe and see Azura in front of you, offering to you the knowing of your own *spaciousness* in celestial *blue*. All is possible within you, for just as the sky has no end, so it is with you. Like a magic carpet, imagination can take you with the speed of lightening to your dreams. And through the universal power that has endless possibilities, you can create those dreams into your reality. Expand and go beyond what you presently can see, for that is your birthright. It is a truth for you.

Breathe into you, like a gentle breeze, the beautiful celestial color of *peach*. With great sweetness and total *contentment*, Harmonee hands it to you. In this space you know that all is well, that all fits together in perfect symmetry and is divinely orchestrated. This knowingness offers an understanding for creating the wholeness you desire and you can see how it all blends together as part of the whole, that there is a reason for everything and you have the faith to accept what you cannot see as yet. In this space you are content, knowing that nothing is amiss, yet knowing you can return to wholeness, which is your heritage. And so it is…Amen.

Abbreviated Visualization of the Next Seven Celestial Lights for Yourself & Others to Heal

As the *purple* celestial light wafts into your being, feel the majestic flow of energy and power that ignites you. Your royal heritage gives credence to your inner strength and fortitude just as a lion stands in its own regal strength as ruler of the animal kingdom. In this color, given by Arielle, the power of truth is revealed. Truth is the essence of your being, for truth is of love. Accepting your power and *magnificence* enables you to radiate outward to others their own magnificence.

Elegantly surging into you now is the celestial light *rose*, brought to you by Megalo. This is the undeniable power of a great divine love within you so that you can project this warmth and power to the world. It is stronger than a mother's love and expresses a *magnetic* charisma that draws to you those who wish to experience this love. It is freely given, with no bindings, and has the power to warm the frozen hearts until their fears melt away. In this lies your mission: the spreading of divine love, so that the world can know balance and beauty once again.

Behold Samantha, richly displaying the celestial light *jade green*. Herein you can see the brilliance of life as a new vital energy fills your being. As you release all that does not serve your highest good, there is a *regeneration* of your soul. Patience is required when passing from the old to the new, and this is being taught to you now. Through this you become stronger beyond your imagination, building a strong foundation that can support many who are weaker. They will reach out to you for they can feel your strength.

In a wisp of imagination appears Starr, offering to you the celestial light of *golden yellow*. It brilliantly *illuminates* the sky and is truly magical. Warmth floods your being now, submerging your soul into a depth of love not known before. As you accept the love of God you are able to give out what resides within you. The world hungers for this love, and you are the light for the world to see. Allow it to shine brilliantly, and there is your glory.

Bring to you now the celestial light of *vibrant blue*. Victor presents it to you, bringing amazing possibilities for you. With the possibilities come courage and valor which are needed to step into the unknowns of life. As a being of light you must be the guide for others who cannot see for their darkness. *Expand* into more and become what you cannot see, for it is waiting for you. Feel yourself propelled into the unknowns where movement provides opportunities of a noble heritage. Continue to lift your eyes higher for there is always more to see. In your vision, others can receive the support they need to take the needed step.

Deep within glows the celestial light *coral*. Open your heart to Salome and accept the *knowingness* that is given now. There is a deep understanding of divine order in which everything flows together with the symmetry of perfection. It is here that you can be present in each moment and know that all is as is meant to be. Peace and calm surround in and about you in this place of knowingness. It is here that you are real, and it is here that all unfolds for your life with complete freedom.

Concluding Celestial Light For This Healing Advancement

Descending on you now is the celestial light of *dove gray*, as Dolcei hands it to you. Like a blanket it covers you with total *bliss*. Flow with the trancelike feeling of spiritual joy that abides within when in this state of bliss. This is your original state, and you can rest in the knowing that although things may seem upturned they are in perfect order. Here you can remain calm when all around you is in turmoil, and this can be shown to the world who does not know this. Embrace this bliss, for in this place is love and truth.

And so it is…Amen

About the Author

Carolyn Porter is an inspirational teacher—keynotes, seminars, speaking and coaching trainings—and an author, wholeness coach and energy facilitator. She is the author of multiple books, ebooks and audios, and her core desire is to remind individuals of their divine heritage, their essence of love, the birthright of power within them, and their worthiness to receive all that is good. Having spent many years following the crowd who live in fear, she understands the pull to that life experience, but also the joyous existence she now has being free to experience life in peace, joy, happiness and abundance, as life is meant to be lived.

It is our wish that this book touches your heart and soul by remembering your own power and greatness, and thus it is an instrument for your own healing.

We invite you to contact us:

Empower Productions, Inc.

500 Brookeshyre Court
Woodstock, GA 30188

PH: 678-445-3309
FX: 770-591-5432

We invite you to visit our website at www.drcarolynporter.com